Smile It's the Customer who pays you!

Copyright Notice

Copyright © 2016 by Gail Crowder, LLC.

All rights reserved. No part of this publication may be reproduced, distributed, or transmitted in any form or by any means, including photocopying, recording, or other electronic or mechanical methods, without the prior written permission of the publisher, except in the case of brief quotations embodied in critical reviews and certain other non-commercial uses permitted by copyright law.

Book Cover – Jamil Ramsey

Interior layout by Jamil Ramsey

Edited by Dieneke Johnson

Published by G.A.I.L Publishing LLC HUwww.gailcrowderinc.com

Publishing Logo design by Marie Mickle

Disclaimer Certain suggestions are made in this book. While these are intended to be helpful to the reader, the reader must assume all risk associated with following any particular suggestion. Therefore, in purchasing this book, the reader agrees that the authors and publisher are not liable or responsible for any injury or damage caused by the use of any information contained herein.

Printed in the United States of America

CONTENTS

	Preface	5
1	Who We Are and What We Do	7
2	Establishing Your Attitude	16
3	Identifying and Addressing Customer Needs	27
4	Generating Return Business	37
5	In-Person Customer Service	46
6	Giving Customer Service over the Phone	54
7	Providing Electronic Customer Service	63
8	Recovering Difficult Customers	70
9	Understanding When to Escalate	78
10	Ten Things You Can Do to WOW Customers Every Time	85

The single most important thing to realize about any enterprise is that there are no results inside its walls. The result of a business is a satisfied customer.

Peter Drucker

Preface

Each and every one of us serves customers, whether we realize it or not. Maybe you're on the frontlines of a company, serving the people who buy your products or service. Perhaps you're an accountant, serving the employees by producing their pay checks and keeping the company running. Or maybe you're a company owner, serving your staff and your customers.

This book will look at all types of customers and how we can serve them better and improve ourselves in the process.

If you get everybody in the company involved in customer service, not only are they "feeling the customer" but they're also getting a feeling for what's not working.
Alice MacDougall

Who We Are and What We Do

Before we get started, we need to think about what is a customer? What customer service is all about? We also need to think about whom in our organization provides customer service. The simple answer to that question is: everyone.

Who Are Customers?

A customer is, in this day and age, anyone who uses a service. Although this has its logical extremes – you will find few people who are overjoyed by the idea of being a customer to a doctor, or their children a customer of their school. Therefore everyone who relies on you to do a job that will have an effect on their life, their job, or their use of a product is technically one of your customers. Above and beyond that there are different echelons of customers – internal and external, corporate and personal, regular and occasional. These are always people that you will be well-advised to keep happy, so customer service is an important – indispensable, one might say – element of any job in which you have customers.

If, for example, you work in one branch of a department store, and receive a call from someone working in a sister branch of the same store wondering if you have in stock a particular item – one which their branch has run out of, for example, then that individual technically, and temporarily, becomes a customer to you. They want something and are hoping that you can deliver it. To do your job the way one would hope, you will go to whatever lengths are possible in order to provide the best service possible to whoever needs it from you.

Of course, the most regular customers tend to be the external customers who provide the "bread and butter" of any business, the regular day-to-day custom that drives the profits and income of a company. It is also these customers who will, by word of mouth and other means bring your business to the attention of other potential customers. Their role in a business's success is essential, and these customers should be the immediate concern of any business. Ensuring that these customers are satisfied will make the difference between success and failure for any company.

External Customers

External customers are anyone outside your company that you interact with — not just the people who buy goods or services from you. External customers are what can be considered 'traditional' customers:

- They take our products and services and pay for them
- They exist 'outside' the confines of our own organization
- They are open to approach from our competitors
- They may not always be dependent upon us for products and services and may switch away to our competitors

Internal Customers

Internal customers include anyone in your organization who relies on you for services, resources, or information.

Providing excellent customer service to internal customers sets a positive tone for all personal interactions. If internal customers receive excellent customer service every day, they will consider this the norm. If they interact with external customers, they are likely to treat those customers the way they have been treated. Excellent customer service, like most types of human behavior, is contagious.

The quality of service you provide to internal customers ultimately affects the quality of service your company provides to external customers. Even if you never interact with someone outside your company, you are still engaged in customer service. An internal customer may look for any of the following:

- Materials
- Information
- Instruction
- Participation
- Assistance

Internal customers are the people in our own organization who are dependent on us for without whom they cannot perform their tasks to maximum efficiency, and this has either a direct or an indirect effect on the external customer.

What Is Customer Service?

Customer service is one of the true business essentials. Everyone remembers the bad customer service they have had, and most will also remember instances of good customer service. The importance of customer service is recognized by all successful businesses, because it is possibly the number one element in customer retention. If you want to ensure that you get repeat business, looking out for the wishes and needs of your customer base is essential. How you go about providing it is up to you, but there are certain elements which remain the same whatever the nature of your business. These are the principles of good customer service.

Whenever a customer makes a purchase, they will have priorities as to what makes their experience a positive one. Obviously the first priority is that they get whatever they have purchased from the point of purchase to their home. If it is a small item that they can take with them, the business's responsibility is to see to it that the item is packaged and presented in a manageable, portable fashion with a minimum of waiting. However, customer service begins before this. When a customer enters the store or the showroom to find what they are looking for, they may require the attention of staff to enable them to find it. Some customers just want to browse. Staff is required to ascertain what a customer wants how they want to go about it and whether they will need any help.

Customer service can be defined as any action you take to ensure that a customer is pleased with the transaction on a long-term basis. This includes "after sales service", which entails ensuring that the customer leaves the point of sale with the item that they were looking for, within the period of time that they intended to spend sourcing it, and then has no problems using it. It is easy enough to ensure a customer goes away from the point of sale with the item they had come to purchase. Ensuring that they are happy going forward may require more care and attention, and this is where after-sales service needs to be at its highest level. Pre-sales, after sales and point-of-sale service are all essential elements of customer service.

Who Are Customer Service Providers?
Given the importance of customer service, it will inevitably be the case that any company will have to place a strong focus on ensuring that the people within the business do their jobs as required. Any commercial enterprise may have several layers of staff responsibility, and the jobs done by these members may vary considerably. What they all have in common is their importance to a business lies in their ability to do what is required, and how it should be done. Just about anyone can get one of these elements right, and most will be able to do two. Customer service providers have to get all three.

In any business, a customer service provider is someone whose performance of their role is important to the overall result for the customer. Most customers will not care much for what happens behind the scenes in a company, so long as they are able to count on their needs being fulfilled. It is therefore the focus of every member of staff to see to it that their job is done without it being necessary for urgent action to be taken. The element of customer service that most customers will notice in any given transaction is that which happens in full view – how the sales people speak to them and how their enquiry is dealt with. But to get to that point, a number of other things also need to be done correctly.

It could be argued that every member of staff within an organization has an element of customer service provision within their responsibilities. It may be something as simple as ensuring that stock is placed where it needs to be placed. It may be something that appears to be entirely divorced from the sales service, such as the work of a security guard who ensures that the store is secure at all times so that everything runs smoothly. One way or another, all of these will impact on the customer experience, and getting it wrong will mean that a company is failing to provide customer service at the level that is expected of them.

Practical Illustration

Dave was applying for a customer service job at a paper selling company. Before he sent in his application, there was a short test. Dave was able to easily recall the information on the types of customers. The internal ones that are buyers within the company, and the external ones that make up the day to day sales of the company. Dave was accepted into the job, and used his skills in customer service to help promote business within the company. He was always kind and honest when helping a customer, and did so in the most efficient way possible. This made it very clear that Dave did indeed deserve the job.

The greatest discovery of my generation is that human beings can alter their lives by altering their attitude of mind
　　　　　　　　　　　　　　William James

Establishing Your Attitude

Customer service means different things to different people. To some it means going beyond what's expected of you. To others it means adding value and integrity to every interaction. To others it means taking care of customers the way you would take care of your grandmother. We might all define customer service a little differently, but we can all agree on one thing: to provide great customer service, you need to put energy and enthusiasm into your interactions with customers. Great customer service begins with a great attitude.

Appearance Counts!

As a society, we are all aware that a lot of emphasis is put on individual appearance. To some extent this is actually something regrettable, as it means that people are prepared to judge a book by its cover. Conversely, however, a company should be aware that the opinions of its customers matter. Those opinions may not be the same as the people working within the company, but when it comes to ensuring the success of a business they still matter. In fact, the saying "the customer is always right" could be considered to apply here. Most customers wish to be treated with courtesy and to deal with individuals who look like they have made an effort with their appearance. Therefore it is beneficial to ensure all staff takes heed of this fact.

This does not mean that in every business it is important for customer-facing staff to be Stepford-style automatons who look, act, and behave as though they had been prepared for their role to ensure that every business operation is the same as the last. A certain amount of character, which includes a modicum of individuality, is desirable in a customer services situation. It is important to maintain standards, but also to give the appearance that each transaction is different from the last.

Even if the transaction or the enquiry is not carried out in person, it is still important to consider the matter of appearance. "Appearance", after all, is not just a term which applies to physical appearance. It also refers to how things *seem*. If a customer is dealing with staff on the phone or via e-mail, they will be well advised to ensure that their professionalism does not slip here. Often in businesses which do not directly face the customer – such as call centers – the dress code is "relaxed". You can wear jeans and a t-shirt, or whatever feels comfortable, as long as your performance is polished and professional. Some businesses prefer to have a strict dress code even in these circumstances, feeling that dressing smartly equates directly to a smart performance.

The Power of a Smile

Often opinions differ on what constitutes a strong approach to customer service. There are some who would argue that efficiency is everything – providing the customer with what they require, when they require it without them needing to ask for it. The overall impression that this method aims for is that things happened without anyone needing to try, as if by magic. This means that courtesy counts for an increasing amount in customer transactions.

Being positive and friendly in customer interactions plays a major part in ensuring that a customer walks away from the experience having felt that everything was done in a way that suggested the customer is valued. This may impact on how much they spend in a single transaction, and just as important, whether they return to the business with more customers, because of their positive experience. In this respect, a smile can make a world of difference to how the customer feels about their treatment, and about the business in general.

Having a smile on your face makes you look more welcoming. It is something that cannot be overestimated as a customer service and retention tool. If you were to walk into a store, and saw two sales assistants – one who looked cheerful and open and one who looked like they had just opened an overdue credit card bill – instinct would dictate that you approached the cheerful one should you have an enquiry about the item you wanted to buy. Therefore it is advised that in dealing with customers you are always alert, friendly, and personable. Even if you are not particularly feeling that way, it has been argued by body language experts that the act of smiling releases endorphins which make you feel happier. So it is worth making the effort to put a smile on your face however you are feeling.

Staying Energized

We all experience low points during the course of the day, but there are ways to boost your energy when it is lagging.

- Take a walk, even if it's just to the restroom.
- Drink a glass of cold water.
- Be sure to eat a good breakfast and lunch.
- Plug into others – being with energized people, keeps you energized!
- Listen to up-beat music.
- Try to stay humorous.

A working day usually stretches from around 8-9 AM and goes on until approximately 5 PM. Though there is some movement in these times, the typical structure of a staff timetable is that a working day will extend to around eight hours, and will involve some short breaks in between times. The importance of this information is that it can be difficult to maintain a positive demeanor for eight hours straight, especially if you are thinking about matters beyond the workplace. Eight hours of appearing positive and upbeat can be the hardest part of a job, without even considering the brass tacks of the job – ensuring that the customers are seen to.

It is essential in this respect that anyone in a customer-facing job approaches their day in a sensible, structured fashion which allows them to get the most out of themselves. Staying energized is often difficult, but as long as you develop a routine for dealing with the difficult events, then you can find a way to deal with even the dreariest day. There will be times during a working day when you would like nothing more than to go and get your jacket and walk out the door. However if we all did that whenever we felt like it, the chances are that we would mostly be out of a job.

It is essential to find something that allows you to break out of the "lows" that anyone will experience during a working day. These lows are common to all of us, and we all have different ways of dealing with them. One of the most commonly used methods of shaking out of this kind of torpor is a "change of scenery". If you have a moment and can leave the shop floor, it is beneficial to get up and go somewhere else for a moment. Maybe it will be something as simple as going to get a drink or get some fresh air. Whatever you do, it should be vastly preferable to scowling at every customer who simply asks you the price of a certain item.

It should also be noticed that making the effort to have breakfast in the morning – even if you feel as though eating is the last thing you want to do – can be of huge benefit. It allows you to maintain energy through the morning, which for many people is the hardest time of say to stay positive. It may be a cliché, but making sure that you don't skip breakfast can go a very long way to keeping you energized through the day.

Staying Positive

We can't control all of the problems and irritations that come up during the day. We can control our attitude and how we react to the situation, remember: you need to be happy with the reflection in the mirror.

Tips on staying positive:

- Rearrange or redecorate your workspace

- View negative situations as a training session for your future, use them to your benefit, they may help you later in life.

- Find ways to spend more time on tasks you enjoy

- Look for opportunities to learn new things

- Realize that you can find positives in any negative situation. Albert Einstein said: *"In the middle of every difficulty lies opportunity."*

At the beginning of the day, think about one important thing that you want to accomplish that day. Think about why it is important. Tell yourself that you have the ability to accomplish it successfully. Congratulate yourself when you have accomplished what you set out to do.

Positivity is something that is very hard to create out of nothing. It occurs naturally in some people, and others are deficient in it. Positivity can result from good things happening at the right time – or for that matter at any time. It can act as an energy source on which a person can access to bring the best results time and again. Whether you are a boss looking for good results from a sales team, or a salesperson looking for your own positive results, it is essential to bear in mind that the best results come from situations where the individual, and those with whom they work, feel that positive energy that feeds into a good performance.

Most of us have spent time with positive and negative people. Although those who are negative may be so for perfectly good reasons – past experience may have seen them consistently fail to get what they want – they can be difficult to deal with, even to the point where they seem to sap the positivity from those who have it in supply. This is something that you will tolerate from a friend, but in a workforce it is essential to stop this kind of negativity by whatever means necessary. Having a bright outlook can be difficult, especially when luck seems to be in short supply, but this is what separates good bosses and workers from bad ones.

Outlook and attitude are essential in any job, but particularly in one where you will be dealing with the public. It may seem that the day is not going your way, and that you are permanently going to be frustrated, but the essential thing to remember is that if you project this mood on to the customers, you will certainly have a bad time sales-wise. Positivity is hard to manufacture out of nothing, so sometimes you have to project it when you are not necessarily feeling it. Eventually, if you keep this faux positivity running for long enough, it will create the conditions for real positivity to take hold and thrive. Of course, if you already feel it so much the better – as far as possible you should share it and allow it to become a prevailing condition.

Practical Illustration

Karen was new to customer service and needed some tips on how to best do her job. She asked a colleague, Terry, for some pointers. Terry first noticed that Karen was dressed more casually. She told her that wearing professional looking clothes are an important part of customer service. Secondly, Terry noticed that Karen was not smiling enough. A smile shows that you excited and motivated to deliver the best quality customer service possible, and makes the customer feel more relaxed, so she advised Karen to smile as often as possible when appropriate. Finally, Terry gave Karen some tips on staying energized such as going for short walks or drinking a cold glass of water. Even listening to upbeat music and keeping positive thoughts. Karen really did benefit from all those helpful tips.

Endeavors succeed or fail because of the people involved. Only by attracting the best people will you accomplish great deeds.
Colin Powell

Identifying and Addressing Customer Needs

The first step in improving customer service is to determine what customer's value in their interactions with your organization. What do they want? What do they need? The most obvious way to find out what customers want and need is to ask them. Businesses spend lots of time and money surveying customers, and they often come up with valuable feedback. But the people on the front lines of customer service, people who interact with customers on a daily basis, can gain useful insights into what customer's value just by listening to them and observing them.

The next step, once you have identified customer needs, is to commit yourself to meeting them. But you can't stop there. To provide exceptional service, you need to go the extra mile to show customers how important they are to your organization.

Understanding the Customer's Situation

Customer needs are usually fairly self-explanatory, at least on a basic level. Judging on the basis of what your business is, there are often only a few things they can possibly be looking for. What is essential, though, is that you allow the customer to communicate their needs to you rather than attempting to tell them what they need. They know what they need, and that's why they are here. Any attempt by you to project something on to them is simply going to be taken in a bad way, and is as likely to hurt your sales as anything. Where you can help them is in explaining how those needs can best be met.

Customers will come in many different forms, and each of these forms will present certain challenges. There will be some customers who are very clear about what they want and need, and will put up with very little sales patter from a salesperson. There are others who have only the vaguest idea of what they want to buy, and will essentially give you a rundown of their needs and ask you to fill in the blanks. There are some who will have a lot of questions, and others who will simply want you to do what they ask. In the first few sentences a customer says to you, you will be able to identify their needs or situation, and can operate from there.

The more time you spend in a customer facing role, the more you will learn about the kinds of customer, and the different needs that they have. You will become adept at learning what a certain customer wants from you, and will be able to identify the way the situation will go without needing to ask too many questions. The benefit of experience is in how it allows you to make quick decisions and satisfy the customer in an efficient and courteous manner. It is often said that there are no bonuses or statistics for customer service, but it is customer service that will bring the most sales and the most repeat business.

Staying Outside the Box

Many people argue that the quickest way of judging a situation is to pre-judge it. Those who trust their instincts to give them the right steer in a situation may often get it right, and find that there is real benefit in doing so. Certainly, the advantages of having good instincts are clearly evidenced by good results in terms of sales. However, it can also be negative to be too quick off the mark in terms of identifying a customer's needs. The results of this course of action can be that you appear either presumptuous or incompetent, and you may even insult the customer by being so bold. It is generally worth allowing the customer a chance to let you know what they want. They may well leave some information incomplete, and this is where your sales instincts can be most useful.

There are many ways you can fall into the trap of presuming too much. Many people tend to judge customers by appearance, and assume that because a customer of the same age, gender or any other grouping tends to want a specific item, that this will necessarily hold true of any customer in that sector. It helps to allow the customer to say what they are going to say first, and then fill in any blanks that are left. It may seem like a neat trick to "know" what the customer wants before they say anything, but when you get it wrong it seems less like a trick and more like a really stupid thing to do. Appearing competent is what's essential.

Apart from any other reason to pause and listen, there is the fact that it is just good manners to do so. Appearing impolite and almost trying to give the impression that you know the customer's needs better than they themselves do, is something that will lose you sales. What you really want to portray is that you have the wisdom to recognize the customer's needs, and the good grace to let them make things clear themselves. You will benefit a lot more from showing consideration than you will from any party tricks.

Meeting Basic Needs
In providing customer service, the priorities of your organization should match the priorities of your customers. At a minimum, you should be sure that you are meeting customers' basic needs.

- **Friendliness**: Friendliness is the most basic of all customers needs, usually associated with being greeted graciously and with a smile. We all want to be acknowledged and welcomed by someone who is glad to see us. A customer should never feel they are an intrusion on your work day.

- **Understanding and empathy**: Customers need to feel that you understand and appreciate their circumstances without criticism or judgment.

- **Fairness**: We all need to feel we are being treated fairly. Customers may get annoyed and defensive when they feel they are subject to unfair treatment.

- **Control:** Control represents the customers' need to feel they have an impact on the way things turn out.

- **Options and alternatives**: Customers need to feel that other avenues are available to getting what they want accomplished. They realize that they may be in unchartered waters, and they depend on us to be "in the know".

- **Information:** Customers need to be educated and informed about our products and services, and they don't want us leaving anything out!

Every customer who steps through the door of your organization, or makes a call to your sales center, provides you with a chance to provide excellent customer service. Every customer will have certain needs that have to be met in order to feel that they can walk away from a transaction satisfied. This is something that the best salespeople and any kind of staff will look to achieve at every opportunity. The customer's needs fall into two main categories – basic needs and specific needs. Whenever the customer comes to the store, they must leave with their basic need satisfied for the transaction not to be considered a failure. The other needs are more negotiable.

Basic needs are those needs which are absolutely essential to the transaction, the customer's reason for coming to the store in the first place. Their basic need may be something quite specific or something vague which they need your help to concretize. A basic need might be something like "I really need a GPS system for my car, can you help?", or equally it could be "I am having problems keeping my car windshield clean, what would you suggest?" Over and above this there may be additional things that they need, but the basic requirement is the thing that they state in their approach to you.

Meeting these needs is absolutely essential, and the important thing is that no matter how large or small those needs are you meet them with the same enthusiasm and manners. You may not get much commission on the sale of a really basic, inexpensive item, but the customer will remember their experience more positively if you are prepared to smile at them and treat their needs as though you consider them every bit as important as any other customer's. The next time they come back, there is every chance that their needs will be for something that costs ten times as much. If they were happy with how you dealt with them before, chances are that they will seek you out again.

Going the Extra Mile

Once you have met that customer's basic needs, what could you do to show that you are committed to providing the best service possible?

Try these simple tasks where applicable:

- Remember someone's name and use it frequently in conversation
- Remember what someone has purchased
- Learn your customers likes and dislikes
- Contact your customers regularly
- Put their needs high on your priority list
- Inform customers of specials and sales
- Be available to meet his/her needs
- Follow up when you say you will
- Be organized and thorough
- Return customer calls promptly
- Demonstrate you want to fulfill their customer needs

Customer service is not just about giving the customer what they ask for. Many people who provide customer services will express the importance of providing to a customer, things over and above what they had asked for – things which, although they may not be "needs" in the sense of things that are absolutely necessary, are certainly nice to have. This is what people call "going the extra mile" – you have taken the transaction to its destination, and now you can take it that little bit further by showing an extra touch to your customer service that the customer will remember the next time they need something.

Going the extra mile is important for the very reason that it is not necessary. The customer will remember the things that someone did for them that were completely unexpected, that another organization or salesperson might not have done. The thing about providing customer service above and beyond is that it allows you to show just how good you are at giving the best customer service. It is easy to provide a certain, expected level of customer service – by many people's estimation it is a minimum consideration. It is the extras that will make the difference, much of the time.

As far as those extras go, it can be something as simple as carrying the item which has been purchased out to the customer's vehicle. It might be something as small as writing a thank you note, to recognize that the customer had a wide range of places to choose from, and appreciate that they chose you. Whatever the case, it is important to consider how you can best provide the customer with not only what they need, but something extra which will stay in their memory for some time.

Practical Illustration

Jenny was a customer service representative for a paper distribution company. She always made sure to meet each customer's needs. She was friendly, and gave the customer options and alternative solutions to their problems when available. She always made them feel in control. Yet when she got back her feedback report, it was good, but not great. She decided to ask her co-worker Debra how to go the extra mile. She mentioned remembering the customer's name and using it frequently, and returning customer calls promptly. After implementing all of Debra's tips, Jenny saw a rise in customer satisfaction in her next feedback report.

There is a place in the world for any business that takes care of its customers — after the sale.

Harvey MacKay

Generating Return Business

People who have been in business for a while know the value of return business. Experts believe that it costs at least five times more to attract new customers than it does to keep existing ones. If you think about the cost of advertising and salespeople, you can see why winning a new customer is so much more expensive.

Your customers are like everyone else. They want to feel appreciated. If they feel that you have forgotten about them as soon as a transaction is complete, they may take their business elsewhere. On the other hand, if you show a genuine interest in keeping in touch with them and meeting their needs, they will keep coming back. We all like to do business with companies we know and trust. You should strive to be that kind of company.

Following Up

Following up after a sale or any customer contact is something that some people consider an optional extra in business. To some people, the idea is to simply provide the customer with what they came for, and let them go on their merry way once they have got it. The priority after this is to go ahead with doing your job in respect to other customers. However, the fact is that a little bit of follow-up work, can make a huge difference to the way your business retains customers, and attracts follow-up business from friends of the original customer.

Follow-up work is a major part of customer services. A customer will always see the good service they got from a business as a reason to return the next time they need something of a similar nature. This kind of service is arguably more powerful than paid advertising as a tool to get customers through the door on a regular basis. Any customer who feels that they have been given exemplary service will be like a walking billboard or a cheerleader for your company. This is something that many companies fail to keep in mind, and it costs them money in the long run.

After the sale, service can take on many forms. It may be the person or persons who are on the spot to provide advice and customer support if the customer has difficulties with the purchased product or service. It may be a call a few weeks after the purchase is made to find out whether the customer is happy with their purchase and whether there is anything more that you can do for them. Showing a customer that they mean something to you and your company is a very important part of giving customer service that is not good, but great.

Addressing Complaints

Customer complaints should always be taken seriously. You can turn a negative situation into a positive by treating complaints as opportunities to show customers how much you care about providing exceptional service.

Customer's Bill of Rights:

- To be taken seriously
- To be listened to
- To be respected
- To receive a quick response

No business, no matter how big or small, likes to have customers complain about the service they have received or the product they have bought. There is something galling about being the subject of a complaint, and no matter how impersonal it is, it still feels almost like a personal slight. The important thing in business is to respond to such a situation with the requisite level of grace. Where the customer goes away raving about what a fabulous level of customer service they have received in adversity, and promising to return when they next need a similar service.

Mistakes happen in life and in business, and so much of what we are about is shown by how we deal with the consequences of these mistakes. The situation which a customer is complaining about may not even have been your error to begin with, but regardless of who made the error, taking ownership of it and dealing with a complaint in a gracious, helpful manner can turn an awkward situation into one which showcases the best of your abilities. There is, in many cases, a tendency to become defensive when someone is complaining – especially if they are doing so in a very forthright manner. Maintaining a professional tone at these times can be difficult, but managing to do it and solve the problem can showcase a positive side of you and the business.

Even if you think the issue about which the customer is complaining is trivial, not a cause for complaint, or not your company's fault, it is wise to give the customer their chance to speak, show that you take them seriously, and offer to do whatever you can. If the problem genuinely turns out to be something you can do nothing about – because of a difficulty with another company's product or the customers understanding of the way the product should work – there may still be something you can do – by placing a telephone call or getting a technician to check out the problem. By showing a commitment to helping customers, you can win some valuable reputation points.

Turning Difficult Customers Around

Over time, you and your coworkers have probably developed some effective ways of dealing with challenges that come up in dealing with difficult customers. Sharing those ideas can benefit everyone.

The seven situations of difficult customers (*and suggested ways of dealing with them*) are:

1. You don't know the answer to a customer's question (Tell the customer that you don't know the answer, but you will find out)

2. You have to say no to a customer's request (Explain why you have to say no; offer alternatives)

3. Your computer is working slowly and the customer is getting impatient (Tell the customer your computer is working slowly; keep the customer informed about what's happening)

4. The customer makes an unrealistic request (Explain what alternatives you can offer)

5. The customers doesn't seem to believe you (Offer to show proof or backup information)

6. The customer is angry (Stay calm; acknowledge the customer's feelings)

7. The customer doesn't want to give you the information you need (Explain why you need the information)

Although the saying goes that the customer is always right, there can often be a lot of space between knowing that the customer is "right" and accepting that they have a point. It can often be extremely frustrating dealing with certain customers, especially those who show limited understanding of your situation. Sometimes, due to the limitations of your job, a customer will present you with a request that you simply cannot deliver on. They may well become insistent on the subject, and in some situations customers have been known to become abusive. Dealing with this as a customer service provider can be difficult, but it is one of those challenges that makes you or breaks you in the role.

Sometimes customers are of the belief that a customer service provider is all-powerful. The belief seems to come from the fact that, as an employee of the company, you will have some access to the inner workings of the company. Frequently the extent of a complaint will be that "this doesn't work and I want a new one/this one to be fixed/my money back". Their displeasure will be clear, and may even shade into anger. Trying to defuse a situation like that is always a challenge, and requires a great deal of patience. It is not impossible, however – and emerging triumphant from such a situation can be a very big milestone.

The important thing to keep in mind when dealing with a customer complaint is that losing your patience with the customer will never lead to a satisfactory conclusion – for you and most likely for them. Although it may seem galling, and rather challenging, you will need to keep a firm hold of your temper and address their complaint to the best of your knowledge and ability. Tell them that you can see their problem and you will do everything you can to make sure it is corrected. Explain to them what you are going to do, and gain their assent for everything before you do it. If there is no way you can help them, do not chase a lost cause. Explain that you cannot help them, explain why, and offer apologies and a word of advice about where they can get help. This can lead to a positive resolution – but if it does not, at least you will have done what you can.

Practical Illustration

Cory worked for a paper distribution company. When Cory got his annual performance report back, and found that he was lacking in sales, he decided that he would need to do something to fix it. He noticed that a lot of customers were unique, so he needed to practice his follow up work to keep them coming back. He checked through his email and voice mail much more frequently, and started calling older customers about new deals and offers the company was now offering. Another thing he noticed was that some of the feedback was less than perfect. He started striving to listen to customer's problems and taking further steps to help resolve the problems and concerns of the customers. After his next report, he noticed increases in sales and also an increase in returning customers. His feedback began improving, and he was back on track.

People don't want to communicate with an organization or a computer. They want to talk to a real, live, responsive, responsible person who will listen and help them get satisfaction.
General George S. Patton

In-Person Customer Service

In-person interactions provide a great opportunity to build rapport with customers. When you talk to a customer on the phone or you exchange emails with a customer, it can be difficult sometimes to get a sense of what the other person is thinking and feeling. But when you talk to a customer in person, you get constant feedback, both verbal and nonverbal. It's easy to tell if you are creating the right impression. Although in-person interactions can be difficult at times, they offer exceptional insight into what customers want and need.

Dealing with At-Your-Desk Requests

Sometimes working in a job that requires customer service will put you on the spot. You can be working hard on something you have had in your planner for days, when suddenly a customer turns up at your desk with a problem. It is common in these situations to wonder if you should go ahead and provide the customer with the help they need – thus missing the work you were scheduled to do – or to try and find a way to get rid of the customer so you can get on with what you need to do. In any case like this, the matter of priority arises.

There is nothing more unprofessional than turning a customer away and saying "Sorry, I'm busy. If you want to come back another time I'm sure I'll be able to fit you in tomorrow/next week/ in ten days' time". The customer has come to see you in person, they consider their problem to be of some importance, and they are relying on you to help them. If the work in hand is really something that cannot wait you have two options. You can find someone else who will be able to do the work, and turn your attention to the customer, or you can find someone to help the customer so that you can get on with your work.

It is vital to keep a sense of courtesy whatever you decide to do. The customer who has come all this way to see you will be somewhat unimpressed if you just ask them to take a seat and assign someone to ask what the problem is. However urgent the work you are doing is, you have enough time to speak to the customer, ask them the nature of their problem, and think about how best to bring about a solution. It may be that the difficulty is one that only you can solve. If, however, you can find someone else to help the customer, make sure that you have taken note of the problem and explain it thoroughly to whoever you delegate the matter to. Also ensure that the person you hand over to is someone who can genuinely solve the problem. Otherwise it will look like you have simply wriggled out of the situation. Courtesy and competence are essential, whoever deals with the problem.

The Advantages and Disadvantages of In-Person Customer Service

For many companies, customer service is something that is the responsibility of a dedicated department which can only be contacted by telephone, post, or in some cases only by e-mail. For others, the reality is that numbers dictate customer service to be something which is provided in person at the point of sale. Being able to provide customer service in person is essential for these companies, however helpful it would be to have a dedicated set of customer service professionals. That said, being forced to provide customer service in person, as time-consuming as it may be, has its advantages in the circumstances. Whatever else can be said about this way of providing customer services, it does allow a level of personal service that is hard to beat.

Speaking to the customer in person rather than on the phone has its drawbacks, and no one would deny this. It keeps professionals away from other work, and can lead to them getting drawn into long, complicated discussions which would be better carried out in a less pressured way. However, when it comes to customer confidence, being able to look a customer in the eye and tell them that you will get to the bottom of their problem does enable a certain amount of satisfaction on the part of the customer that is not easy to achieve in any other way.

When dealing with customer service issues on the telephone, it is possible – and sometimes irresistible – to put the customer on hold and transfer them to someone else. Anyone who has been the customer in this situation knows how frustrating that can be, especially when they then have to relate their problem to another person because it has been poorly communicated. Good customer services rely on being able to maintain the confidence of the customer, assure them that their problem will be solved now, and at no extra cost to them. It also allows a personal touch which is hard to achieve any other way, and when it comes to customer retention and future business, a friendly face will have a lot more impact than a disembodied voice or a few lines of text.

Using Body Language to Your Advantage

In any in-person interaction, body language has a major effect on how people interpret your message and respond to it.

Types of body language:

- Eye contact
- Facial expression
- Posture
- Gestures
- Nodding (or shaking your head "no")

Body language is a controversial topic. There are many people who will swear blind that, whatever anyone else says, the only kind of language that can be trusted is that which is spoken and is written down. However, there are many dedicated body language experts who have made clear and incontrovertible findings that make clear the truth about body language. It is said for a reason that it is possible to lie with your words, but never with your eyes. Whatever you can say to a person vocally, it is always better to be able to back it up by looking them in the eye and making a statement that they can trust.

Body language is honest in many ways because it happens by accident. When you are speaking to someone, you are likely to be doing things with your body that you do not even realize you are doing. Ask any seasoned poker player and they will tell you that – in a game which uses few words – the way they know what another player is going to do, and what hand they have, is by looking at their hands, their face and their body. Some people touch their face or tug their collar when they are lying. Someone at ease will sit back in their seat and be more open in their posture. A person under pressure will look around themselves more.

Whatever you say to a customer, it is important to use body language to your advantage. The way you conduct yourself in the presence of a customer may well have more impact on their confidence in you than anything you say to them. If you look around you when they are relating a problem, it will give them the impression that you do not care and only want them to get it off their chest and leave you alone. If you look at them and nod when they say something of importance, they will take from that that you are listening to them and are interested in seeing that their problem gets solved. Retaining a customer's confidence is essential, and your use of body language will dictate how successful you are in doing that.

Practical Illustration

Korra had been busy all week. She had a huge report due the next day and she had fallen a bit behind. A customer named Matt came in with a complaint about an order he had placed that had never been delivered. Korra's first thought was to tell him she was too busy to help and to come back later, but she knew that would never do. Instead she looked to see if anyone else could help him out. The only people that weren't up to their necks in paper work were not a part of customer service. One of them offered to finish up the report so that Korra could help the customer. In a few moments, Korra had successfully helped the customer track down the source of the problem and had his goods finally delivered.

Every great business is built on friendship.

J.C. Penney

Giving Customer Service over the Phone

When you are talking to someone in person, body language makes up a large part (some would say more than half) of your message. But as soon as you pick up the phone, body language becomes irrelevant. The success of your interactions depends almost entirely on your tone of voice and your choice of words. Getting these things right isn't easy, but with a little practice anyone can learn how to provide excellent customer service over the phone.

The Advantages and Disadvantages of Telephone Communication

As has previously been mentioned, many companies place their customer service issues in the hands of a dedicated department who can only be contacted in a non-personal manner. Some companies do this by using e-mail and others by way of the mail. In most cases, however, a customer service department will do the bulk of their work over the phone, and will have a dedicated call center for this purpose. While this removes the personal element from customer service to a large extent, it would be inaccurate to claim that there is not an advantage to doing things this way. Quite apart from anything else, it does permit some thinking time that you might not get in person.

The main disadvantage to this way of doing things is that there is no allowance made for the fact that people are almost always more reassured by speaking to someone in person. The body language we use when trying to transmit reassurance and confidence relies on customers being able to see us. If they relate a problem to you, and you are silent while they do so (for obvious reasons of manners and courtesy), they may understandably wonder if you are actually listening. The only way to avoid this becoming a problem is to be as reassuring in your tone of voice as you can. Make clear to the customer that you understand the severity of the situation, and that you will do all you can to solve it.

Even with this level of understanding there are some customers who will feel that things will take longer to get solved over the phone, and the moment they hang up their problem will be forgotten about. This is why you must explain to them at each stage of the process what you are doing; why you are doing it and what will happen next. Solving the problem in the course of one call may be impossible, and you may have to promise them that they will be called back. Some companies make promises like this and signally fail to follow through on them. This can lead to a loss of confidence in all companies who make promises and a resultant pressure on those who are good at problem solving. Solving problems over the phone takes dedication and perseverance. Doing the job well and promptly will pay dividends.

Telephone Etiquette

Customers expect a courteous, helpful response when they call your business. Reviewing the basics of telephone etiquette can remind you about what it takes to provide the kind of response that customers expect.

Telephone etiquette:

- Answer promptly, on the third ring at the latest.
- Before you pick up the phone, end any conversation you are having.
- Greet the caller, identify yourself, and ask if you can help.
- Speak clearly in a pleasant tone of voice. Avoid speaking too quickly. (For discussion: what message do you send if you speak too quickly?)
- Give the caller time to explain the reason for the call. Don't interrupt. Don't sound like you're in a hurry.
- When you need to put someone on hold, ask first: "Can I put you on hold for just a minute?" After you return to the line, thank the customer for holding.
- If you need to transfer a call, explain what you're doing.
- When you end a call, let the customer hang up first. This will ensure that you don't cut the customer off prematurely.

Telephone etiquette is a major issue in any company that conducts a lot of its business and its customer service over the phone. The main factors in telephone etiquette are, as the words suggest, manners and efficiency. Because most of our conversations are carried out in person, a lot of people feel quite ill-at-ease when speaking on the phone. Things that they would normally be able to rely on for reassurance, like eye contact and body language, are not easily translated to a phone conversation. It means that dealing with urgent business on the phone can be something of a minefield.

If you are required to provide a lot of your customer services over the phone, it is essential that you pay attention to your telephone manner. If you are receiving a call, this will mean responding promptly, and making your opening greeting courteous and warm. Rather than simply saying "Hello?" or saying the name of your company, you should state the name of the company, your name, and ask how you can help. No matter how many times you have done this, do not race through it and make it sound robotic – it may be commonplace to you, but to the customer this is an important matter.

The fact that the customer cannot see you when you are on the phone does not mean that you can do whatever you like while you are speaking to them. If you are reading something or waving to a friend while on the telephone, it will be clear from your voice that your full attention is not on the call. If, for any reason, you have to speak to someone in the office, first ask the customer to bear with you, and then place them on hold. It is insulting to leave the customer hanging as though they are less important than what you are doing, and this is compounded by leaving them to hear what you are saying to someone else – the impression given is "it doesn't matter, it's only a customer". Because the customer cannot see what you are doing, it is important to keep them posted on what you are doing. If you do not, they will become agitated.

Tips and Tricks

For some people, dealing with issues over the phone will never be as beneficial as doing it in person. There are many advantages to using the telephone, and in many cases this has led to over-reliance on the system. This in turn has led to us almost developing a specific form of language when we are on the phone, all the more so in a business setting. Remember though that a customer may not be party to this language, and that they will have difficulty keeping up with the conversation if you are not careful to keep their needs in mind. Below are some hints to make your telephone etiquette in a business setting as good as it possibly can be.

- Answer the phone by saying "hello" or "good morning." Often callers don't hear the first thing you say. If the first thing you say is your name, some people might not catch it.

- Smile. Yes, of course, the customer can't see you, but smiling gives your voice a more cheerful, enthusiastic tone. It also reminds you to be upbeat and positive.

- Sound enthusiastic. Try to maintain a positive attitude and let that come through in your voice.

- Say your name and your phone number clearly. Because people say these things often, they tend to slur them. But these are the things that you need to say as clearly as possible!

- Avoid company jargon (such as acronyms).

- Avoid technical terminology as much as possible. Some people may feel reluctant to ask you to explain a technical term because they don't want to seem like dummies.

- Stay alert to how the customer is responding. Does the customer sound confused, skeptical, unsatisfied?

- Don't use a speaker phone unless you're having a conference call. When you use a speaker phone, callers get the impression that you're too busy (or you consider yourself too important) to give them your full attention.

- Say good-bye. Don't end a call abruptly. You will sound like you're trying to get rid of the customer.

- If you need to make notes about the call, do that right away. Don't rely on your memory to reproduce information accurately.

Practical Illustration

Perry was the new sales representative for a paper distribution company. He made his first call, and answered with a greeting. He explained the company he was representing and what services were offered. All the while, he tried to maintain a pleasant and upbeat tone by smiling even though the customer couldn't see it. He continued making calls like this, but ran into a snag. Apparently, Perry was not saying his name and phone number clear enough, so customers couldn't contact him. He made sure to slow down his speech in order to speak more clearly. After a while, it became apparent that he was a natural, and all his techniques were a success!

*About 70% of customers' buying decisions are based on positive human interactions with sales staff.
People buy from people, not companies.*

Lee J. Colan

Providing Electronic Customer Service

A growing number of customer interactions are taking place online. Younger people in particular prefer to do too much of their business online rather than in person. But online interactions have limitations. To provide excellent customer service online, you need to understand what works and what doesn't work, and how to make the most of the tools that are available to you.

The Advantages and Disadvantages of Electronic Communication

Electronic communication is something which has taken off in a big way in today's society. Most people now are familiar with e-mail, text messaging, instant messaging, and social networking sites such as Facebook and Twitter. Each of these forms of communication has definite advantages, but it is worth remembering that, relatively speaking, these forms are in their infancy. Many of us may have been e-mailing for a decade or more now, but people have been using the telephone for much longer, writing letters for longer than that, and speaking directly (one way or another) since mankind began. There are many people who have become very used to doing things in the "old" ways, and who are not yet on the same page when it comes to electronic communication.

The advantages of e-mail are very obvious. Firstly, it is highly convenient. Unlike sending a letter, e-mail gets there instantly. If someone is looking for a detailed, same day response and cannot get to the telephone at the same time as you, e-mail is absolutely wonderful as a way of getting the information across. As well as this, a telephone call costs a certain amount per minute. However long you make your e-mail message, it will cost the same to send as a three-line update. Once it is sent, it stays in the recipient's inbox until such time as they read it and then decide what action to take.

However, as has been mentioned with telephone conversations, there is a body of opinion which holds that e-mail is a very impersonal and cold way of communicating. Certainly if someone wishes to pass on news that may be sensitive, e-mail is not the best way to go about it. A telephone conversation leaves us relying on the inflection in our voice to give the correct interpretation to the words (in the absence of body language) – and in e-mail, we don't even have that inflection to rely on. Therefore, e-mail does have its benefits and cannot be dispensed with entirely as a way of providing customer service, but its limitations need to be understood.

Understanding Netiquette

With the massive changes that the Internet has brought to many of our lives, it is entirely unsurprising that it has brought another substantial change – that which it has wrought on the English language – and most other languages too. New words have been invented – and new uses found for old words – in order to describe things which simply did not exist before the Internet came along and changed our world. A decade ago, pretty much no-one "blogged", absolutely no sane human being Tweeted, and the word "netiquette" was unknown. Not only do we have to mind our Ps and Qs, we would be well advised to keep an eye on our @s as well.

If we are required to contact a customer by e-mail, it is important to be aware that the usual standards pertaining to e-mail do not apply. Many, if not most, people, have a different way of expressing ourselves in e-mail than we would if we were writing a letter or speaking on the telephone. Perhaps emboldened by the text messaging revolution, many people have taken the "txt spk" approach to writing e-mails. Even though e-mail is not bound by the character limits that text messaging and Twitter impose upon us, people will still try to squeeze a message into a few short lines and cut words down. But when using e-mail in a business setting, it is essential to avoid this, as it is seen as being unprofessional.

Tips and Tricks

Because so much of what we do on the Internet has been molded from the social aspect, which makes the medium great fun for most of us, the process of electronic communication has become more influenced by that social aspect. When we are communicating with customers it is essential to remember that things are different. We all have different ways of expressing ourselves in person, on the phone, and the Internet. The issue of how to correctly express oneself in online communications will be somewhat different from the traditional ways.

Electronic communication is disembodied, and specifically e-mail can come across as being extremely abrupt. Even phrases like "thank you" "have a great time" and even "I love you" can seem quite straight and lifeless when placed in a standard font on a computer screen. It is essential to avoid this abruptness in a customer service e-mail. Picking your words carefully is essential, avoiding jargon is fundamental, and it must be remembered that brevity in what you say should be limited to simply saying things in the simplest way. Abbreviations are not for this kind of e-mail.

When we speak out loud, our words have an inflection, they are absorbed by the listener, and then we move on. In an e-mail, it stays there on the page and can be read into a number of different ways. It is essential to avoid saying things that are ambiguous, as this can lead to a complaint some way down the line if misinterpreted. Remember that in person if you say something, the listener can then respond instantly before you move on to your next point. This means that if something you said was unclear, they can seek clarification before replying. In e-mail, this is not possible. Getting things said clearly and unambiguously – and ideally just once – is hugely important.

Eliminate Electronic Ping Pong

One of the benefits of e-mail is its promptness. Sending an e-mail to a friend, a customer, or a co-worker can be done very quickly, and will usually be read within a short time of being sent. This system means that, wherever our conversation partner is in the world, we can converse in real time without the need for a huge telephone bill. Partially due to this, we have a habit of sending e-mails in a very cursory manner, which can lead to them being sent with information missing. This leads to a phenomenon known as "electronic ping-pong", with each party sending ten e-mails to each other to organize or clarify something that could have been handled in the space of two or three messages.

Practical Illustration

Jeremy wanted to report the high lights of a seminar he recently attended to a foreign business colleague. Letters were far too slow, and because of the time zone differences, it was very inconvenient to the both of them to try and call. He instead decided to break out his laptop and send an email. He paid careful attention to his spelling and such, as he tended to shorten word and phrases out of habit. Once he was done drafting it, he emailed it to his colleague later that night. By morning, he had a reply from the other side of the world, all through the power of electronic communication.

Your most unhappy customers are your greatest source of learning.

Bill Gates

Recovering Difficult Customers

One of the hardest challenges customer service staff face is dealing with difficult customers. Sometimes customers have a legitimate reason to be upset and sometimes they don't. In either case, customer service staff needs to be prepared for dealing with difficult customers and finding ways to win them back.

De-Escalating Anger

No matter which method you are using to provide customer service, it is almost inevitable that at times you will have to deal with an angry customer. This is the case in even the best-run businesses, and for the best customer service individuals. Sometimes, whether justifiably or otherwise, customers will get annoyed with the company and will wish to vent that anger at the first available representative. It will frequently be quite powerful anger which may boil over into verbal abuse, but the job of a customer service provider is to accept that it will happen and get on with solving the problem. The first step in doing this is to try and calm the customer down; because it will be difficult to solve a problem if they are boiling with fury, whether their anger is justified or not.

The first thing you must do is speak to the customer in a calm manner and get straight the nature of the problem. It may be the case that they want to scream and shout a bit to vent their fury, and it is up to you how long you give them to do this. Your opening gambit should be something along the lines of "I can tell this is obviously a matter of some importance to you – I'd like to do what I can to help you". Saying "please, calm down" or refusing to help until they have stopped shouting will simply escalate their anger.

Very often, anger arises as the result of a misunderstanding. In these cases it is essential to get to the source of the misunderstanding as quickly as possible. You should speak to the customer and allow them to see that you realize the matter is important. Do not say "I understand" or "I sympathize" – they do not want your sympathy and they will doubt that you understand. Getting the problem laid out, so that you can move forward, depends on getting the customer to see that you are willing to help. From that point, they will be a lot more ready to calm down and proceed.

Establishing Common Ground

When your job entails dealing with customers, it is inevitable that from time to time some of those with whom you deal will be dissatisfied and in something of a mood. Your job in this case – as in all cases of customer service – is to ensure that the issues are dealt with promptly and efficiently. If this should mean that you have to listen to some ranting first of all, then it is worth accepting that this will be the case, and allowing a customer to say what they feel they have to say before getting to the heart of the problem. When all is said and done, you will be seeking to get the point across to the customer that you both have a common goal – the resolution of their problem.

It stands to reason, as a result of the circumstances, that the customer will display signs of anger towards you initially. You, to them, are a symbol of the company for whom you work, which is also the company with which they have an issue. In the customer's eyes, you will be an opponent, and someone to be overcome. Your task is seeing to it that they realize that this is not the case. You are both on the same side here, as people who want to find an end to their problem. Of course they will not see it that way at the beginning and this is where you will need to employ good customer service. Ask questions about the problem, to demonstrate that you are taking it seriously. Begin to formulate a solution and explain what that will be. Allow the customer to be part of this process, and you will gain their confidence.

In the long run, what you are looking for is a solution that the customer will be happy with. They may have begun your interaction by making known their dissatisfaction and being somewhat hostile towards you, but the fact of the matter is that as long as you maintain a calm demeanor and address their problem seriously, looking to work with them as you go, they will recognize you as an ally rather than an adversary, and will be a lot more ready to work with you on the issue. Once the issue is solved, they will remember you as a person who helped them, and will see you and the company in a more positive light.

Setting Your Limits

Sometimes a customer will come to you with a problem that you cannot solve. As a customer service representative it is often expected that you will have the solutions to all problems with your company's products or services at your fingertips. Of course this simply is not possible. Sometimes a customer will come to you with a problem that simply is insoluble, and you will have to tell them so. In these cases it can be difficult to get your point across in a way that leaves the customer satisfied and seeing your point of view – but it is important to at least try.

There are many possible reasons why you may be unable to help a customer with their problem. It may be that they are simply being unreasonable – a defect may have occurred with a product that they bought because they used it for an application it wasn't meant to perform. It may be that the product for which they are seeking help is now obsolete and that the problem is impossible to repair. In either case, the fact remains that you will not be able to grant their request, and you will need to communicate this in a way that allows them to leave on good terms.

So much of human interaction is in how you say things, and customer service is much the same. If you cannot solve a problem, then it is essential to explain why this is the case, and to give the customer all the help possible to find an alternative solution. The more you can do for them along these lines, the more they will understand that, although you could not solve the problem then and there, you gave it your best and you provided them with some help. Demonstrating that you are willing to do what is possible will win you points in almost every case.

Managing Your Own Emotions

When dealing with a customer who is angry, it can sometimes be difficult to maintain your own composure in the face of their protests. Your job as a customer service provider is to try and solve their problem and to avoid getting agitated yourself. However, the fact is that we are all human and we all have our limits and Achilles heels. Sometimes you may well feel that you want to respond to a customer's goading by getting angry at them. This should be avoided as it escalates the situation. Instead you should try to remain calm and bring the customer towards your level of calm.

In many cases, the extent of the customer's anger will be that they have had a problem with one of your products and they want to see it repaired. They will be angry because they spent money on something which, in their view, was not worth it. Your job in this case is to try and calm them down by allowing them to see that you will do whatever you can to help them. Rather than being a faceless, nameless representative of a company which has given them a problem, you are a human being. As much as possible, you should present this human face when talking to a dissatisfied customer; manage your emotions, and although it may be difficult it is worth doing.

Sometimes customers will seek to provoke a reaction from you, as they enjoy arguing the point and feel that seeing you get angry will prove that they are right. Try putting yourself in the shoes of the customer, think about how you would respond to such a situation, what you would want to hear? Reaching an understanding may take time and effort, but it is worth doing – particularly as getting angry can lead to getting fired.

Practical Illustration

Jordan had thought he had seen it all, but boy, he was wrong. One morning a very unhappy customer came through the office shouting and demanding help. Jordan was the only customer service representative that wasn't currently busy, so he had to deal with the man. The angry customer was shouting, but Jordan remained calm and collected. Jordan explained that he would try to help him in any way he could. The man eventually calmed down enough to have a discussion, and the issue was resolved rather quickly. It was a simple misunderstanding, and was dealt with accordingly. Jordan was proud of the way he handled the situation, but would rather not have to go through it again anytime soon.

Letting your customers set your standards is a dangerous game, because the race to the bottom is pretty easy to win.

Seth Godin

Understanding When to Escalate

Providing great customer service does not mean that you have to put up with threats, intimidation, or vulgar language from customers. If customers are out of control, you need to take over the situation and protect yourself.

Dealing with Vulgarity

Showing anger, for many people, involves expressing themselves using language which would be considered "vulgar". What one person considers being vulgar may not be considered vulgar by the next person, however there are certain words and phrases which it is agreed are to be avoided in polite conversation. When making a complaint, customers should realize that it is wise to avoid such words and phrases, as it is no more likely to get their problem solved. However, the fact remains that sometime people will resort to such expressions of anger, and as a customer service provider it is up to you to decide what you will allow and what you won't.

The danger of allowing a customer to use a mild profanity without passing comment on it is that they will possibly decide that anything goes. If they can get away with a mild swear word, they may try their luck with something more graphic and insulting. It is wise, even if you are not offended by profanity, to advise them that you cannot continue the conversation if they are going to use profanities. The danger otherwise is that they can begin to outdo themselves.

It is not about what personally offends you. There are many of us who are not in the least offended by swearing, and there are probably few who have not used at least a mild swear word in a moment of pain, frustration, or anger. However, using them towards people is different – you do not know how every person will react, and it is a simple matter of politeness to keep language clean when dealing with official issues. Develop your own policy with profanity from customers, but always bear in mind that there are other customers around, and to allow swearing to continue or escalate does not affect just you.

Coping with Insults

Insults are never nice to hear, particularly when we feel that they are undeserved. When a customer begins to be insulting towards you, it can be embarrassing and it is always uncalled for. Very often, the insult will be prompted more by what you are than by who you are – they will be insulting the company by directing the insult at you – but it is no less unpleasant as a result. While some swear words are insults, not all insults are swear words, and while a profanity may not offend you it may well be the case that an insult will contain no profanity but some extremely personal jibes.

The simple fact is that you are not paid to listen to abuse. If a customer has insulted you it is up to you how you will react, but as with profanity it is worth remembering that, should they get away with one insult they may feel emboldened to go further. Because most companies and individuals have a policy of not dealing with a customer who behaves in an insulting way, a customer who becomes insulting can be considered to have left aside any legitimate complaint and settled for a tirade. You may demand an apology before continuing, or you may immediately refuse to deal any further with the customer. It is unwise, to simply let an insult go and behave as if the customer deserves of the same respect another customer would get.

As with swearing, it is wise to consider other customers in the case of a customer behaving insultingly. One frequent outcome of insults being traded or directed is that things escalate to a more confrontational pitch – something which will make customers nervous and often afraid. As you have to consider customers' comfort it is therefore essential that you do not allow an atmosphere of hostility to persist.

Dealing with Legal and Physical Threats

Legal and physical threats from angry customers are both serious, but they call for different types of response.

How to respond to legal threats:

- Do not attempt to offer your own interpretation of the legal issues involved.

- Tell the customer that you are not in a position to speak for your company on legal matters (unless you are).

- Inform your supervisor immediately.

How to respond to physical threats:

- When a customer makes a physical threat, your number one priority is to protect yourself and your coworkers.

- Get help immediately, either from your coworkers or from security personnel.

- Inform your supervisor immediately.

Occasionally in a situation where a customer feels that their complaint has not been dealt with satisfactorily, they will decide to bring out the "big guns". Depending on the way the customer's mind works, this may be via the means of threats of legal action, or threats of a more physical nature. The two types of threat differ significantly. Where legal threats are concerned, it is somewhat possible that they might have reason on their side. It is unwise in these cases to get into a legal argument with the customer – you are not there to debate issues, but to look for solutions. It is wise simply to state that you are not in a position to comment on legal matters, but that you will pass their message on.

Where physical threats are concerned, it is a different matter entirely. While a legal threat may have some basis in case law, no customer has a right to threaten or direct personal violence towards any member of staff. Physical and verbal assault are both illegal and should be treated seriously. Even if your instinct is to respond to a threat by fronting up to the customer and stating that you doubt their seriousness or capability, it should be resisted as this can be considered provocation. You should always report an instance of any physical threat. Someone who threatens you might threaten anyone else – and no matter how much of a fake and a coward you judge them to be, they might follow through on a threat.

In both cases, your supervisor should be advised of the threat that has been made. If the threat is physical, the last thing you want is for a potentially violent individual to be in the general area when you or your co-workers are leaving work. However much you may doubt their ability to make good their threat, they cannot be allowed to make other people's lives uncomfortable.

Practical Illustration

Kevin was the only sales representative available at the paper distribution company he worked for at the time. He was nearly ready to leave his shift, but an angry customer came in demanding help. The customer insisted he had been wronged in the utmost degree, and that he would pursue legal action against the company. Kevin heard him out and thought his claim would be unjustified, but instead only told the customer that he was not responsible for the company's legal matters. The customer only got more upset, and called Kevin a rude insult. Kevin informed the man that he did not have to continue to help a customer that insults him, and left for the end of his shift, thankful to be away from the man.

Here is a simple but powerful rule — always give people more than what they expect.

Nelson Boswell

Ten Things You Can Do to WOW Customers Every Time

Meeting the basic needs of customers is only the first step in providing great customer service. If you want to make a lasting impression on customers, you need to go the extra mile. Giving customers more than they expect will not only keep them coming back, but it will also inspire to tell their friends about the great service they received.

Ten Tips

Getting customer service right is no easy matter. This is why the companies who are good at it have such a good record of customer retention. It takes time to build a reputation for good customer services. It also takes dedication and people skills.

Here are ten tips to getting customer service right:

1. Greet customers with a smile, either in person or on the phone. It may sound corny, but it's true that customers can hear the smile in your voice when you talk on the phone.

2. Be helpful, even if there's no profit in it. Make customers feel that your primary concern is being helpful to them, whether or not you are actually going to sell them something.

3. Know your product or service. If customers feel that you don't have the knowledge they need, they will look for someone else who does. Your expertise is part of the value you bring to customer interactions.

4. Don't make customers feel like dummies. Of course you know more than your customers do about your product or service, but don't make them feel inadequate because they don't share your expertise.

5. Listen to customers. In dealing with customers, listen more than you talk.

6. Remember that employees will treat customers the way they are treated by management. If employees are treated with consideration and respect, they will be more likely to treat customers the same way.

7. Make customers feel important and appreciated. When a customer needs help, set aside what you're doing, and focus on the customer.

8. Make things easy for customers. Think about how you can make every transaction as fast and effortless as possible for customers.

9. Throw in something extra. Giving customers a little more than they've paid for, or a little more than they expect, can make them feel that you really care about their business.

10. Say thank you. This might seem obvious, but it's easy sometimes to forget to thank customers for their business. A genuine "thank you" can go a long way toward creating good feelings in customers.

Practical Illustration

Jamie worked for a paper distribution company as a customer service representative. Every day at work, Jamie tried to put her best foot forward. One day, a customer came in with a strange complaint. They were angry about the packaging the paper came in, saying that they ordered smaller packages of paper than were delivered. Jamie not only resolved the matter, but also stayed overtime when her shift ended. When the matter was resolved, she made a follow-up call to make sure everything was going smoothly, and left a lasting impression on the customer based on her dedication and persistence.

It is wise to keep in mind that neither success nor failure is ever final.
Roger Babson

Gail's Closing Thoughts

- Quality in service or product is not what you put into it. It is what the client or customer gets out of it.

- Biggest question: Isn't it really "customer helping" rather than customer service? And wouldn't you deliver better service if you thought of it that way?

- The longer you wait, the harder it is to produce outstanding customer service.

www.ingramcontent.com/pod-product-compliance
Lightning Source LLC
Chambersburg PA
CBHW071202090426
42736CB00012B/2424